ORTS

SNOWBOARDING

D1567091

by Mari Schuh

AMICUS | AMICUS INK

snowboard

rail

Look for these words and pictures as you read.

goggles

boot

Zoom! A snowboarder speeds down the slope. He is fast!

A rider is on the halfpipe.

He jumps. He spins.

snowboard

Do you see the snowboard?
The rider rubs wax on it.
Wax makes it slide fast!

Do you see the boot?
It fits into bindings.
These straps hold the
boot on the board.

boot

Do you see the rail?
A rider hops up.
He slides down it.

rail

goggles

Do you see the goggles?
The lenses are tinted.
They keep out the sun.

A rider does a full spin.
She is high in the air! Wow!

snowboard

Do you see the snowboard?
The rider rubs wax on it.
Wax makes it slide fast!

Do you see the rail?
A rider hops up.
He slides down it.

rail

snowboard

rail

Did you find?

goggles

boot

goggles

Do you see the goggles?
The lens is tinted.
They keep out the sun.

Do you see the boot?
It fits into bindings.
These straps hold the
boot on the board.

boot

spot

Spot is published by Amicus and Amicus Ink
P.O. Box 1329, Mankato, MN 56002
www.amicuspublishing.us

Library of Congress Cataloging-in-Publication Data
Names: Schuh, Mari C., 1975- author.
Title: Snowboarding / by Mari Schuh.
Description: Mankato, Minnesota : Amicus/Amicus Ink, [2020] |
Series: Spot sports | Audience: Grades: K-3.
Identifiers: LCCN 2018037408 (print) | LCCN 2019001107
 (ebook) | ISBN 9781681517346 (pdf) | ISBN 9781681516523
 (library binding) | ISBN 9781681524382 (pbk.)
Subjects: LCSH: Snowboarding--Juvenile literature.
Classification: LCC GV857.S57 (ebook) | LCC GV857.S57 S23
 2020 (print) | DDC 796.939--dc23
LC record available at https://lccn.loc.gov/2018037408

Printed in China

HC 10 9 8 7 6 5 4 3 2 1
PB 10 9 8 7 6 5 4 3 2 1

For Lilly of Mankato, Minnesota
—MS

Wendy Dieker, editor
Deb Miner, series designer
Aubrey Harper, book designer
Holly Young, photo researcher

Photos by 4x6/iStock cover,
16; mel-nik/iStock 1, 6–7;
molchanovdmitry/iStock
3; Choups/Alamy 4–5;
carophotos069474/Newscom 8–9;
Harry How/Getty 10–11; Alexey
Savchuk/Shutterstock 12–13;
StockShot/Alamy 14–15

SNOWBOARDING